The Persian Corridor in World War II: The History of the Allies' Most Important Supply Route

By Charles River Editors

A picture of Indian soldiers with a supply convoy headed for the Soviets

About Charles River Editors

Charles River Editors provides superior editing and original writing services across the digital publishing industry, with the expertise to create digital content for publishers across a vast range of subject matter. In addition to providing original digital content for third party publishers, we also republish civilization's greatest literary works, bringing them to new generations of readers via ebooks.

Sign up here to receive updates about free books as we publish them, and visit Our Kindle Author Page to browse today's free promotions and our most recently published Kindle titles.

Introduction

A picture of a British supply convoy in the region

"I would like to express my candid opinion about Stalin's views on whether the Red Army and the Soviet Union could have coped with Nazi Germany and survived the war without aid from the United States and Britain. First, I would like to tell about some remarks Stalin made and repeated several times when we were "discussing freely" among ourselves. He stated bluntly that if the United States had not helped us, we would not have won the war. If we had had to fight Nazi Germany one on one, we could not have stood up against Germany's pressure, and we would have lost the war." – Nikita Khrushchev

In March 1941, President Franklin D. Roosevelt signed the Lend-Lease Act, which authorized the president to give arms to any nation if it was in America's national interest. With that, America was able to support Great Britain without declaring war on Nazi Germany or Italy and thereby officially embroiling the country in World War II. Roosevelt convinced Congress to send aid to Great Britain on the basis that the U.S. would be defending four essential freedoms, and in August 1941, Roosevelt went so far as to secretly meet British Prime Minister Winston Churchill off the coast of Canada, after which the two issued the Atlantic Charter, a statement of Allied goals in the war. It largely reiterated the kind of ideals put forth by Woodrow Wilson a generation earlier, but it also specified that an Allied victory would not lead to territorial expansion or punitive punishment, clearly hoping to avoid what happened at Versailles at the end of World War I. Neutrality was officially over, but war was not yet on for the Americans.

Though Roosevelt could not have known it at the time, the Lend-Lease Act would quickly come to include an altogether different country than Britain. In the warm predawn darkness of June 22, 1941, 3 million men waited along a front hundreds of miles long, stretching from the Baltic coast of Poland to the Balkans. Ahead of them in the darkness lay the Soviet Union, its border guarded by millions of Red Army troops echeloned deep throughout the huge spaces of Russia. This massive gathering of

Wehrmacht soldiers from Nazi Germany and its allied states – notably Hungary and Romania – stood poised to carry out Operation Barbarossa, Hitler's surprise attack against the country of his putative ally, Soviet dictator Joseph Stalin.

Though Germany was technically Russia's ally, Stalin had no delusions that they were friends. Instead, he used this time to build up his forces for what he saw as an inevitable invasion. Initially, Stalin believed he had several years to build up his army before Germany would invade, figuring it would at least take the Germans that long to conquer France and Britain. However, when France fell quickly in 1940, it seemed he might have miscalculated. The British were able to prevent a German invasion thanks to the Battle of Britain in late 1940, and Stalin knew that if he could delay an invasion through the summer 1941, he would be safe for another year. Unfortunately for Stalin, Molotov's mission to Berlin failed and Hitler began to plan to invade Russia by May 1941. Since military secrets are typically the hardest to keep, Stalin soon began to hear rumors of the invasion, but even when Winston Churchill contacted him in April 1941 warning him that German troops seemed to be massing on Russia's border, Stalin remained dubious. Stalin felt even more secure in his position when the Germans failed to invade the following May.

What Stalin did not realize was that Hitler had simply over stretched himself in Yugoslavia and only planned to delay the invasion by a few weeks. The Soviets were so caught by surprise at the start of the attack that the Germans were able to push several hundred miles into Russia across a front that stretched dozens of miles long, reaching the major cities of Leningrad and Sevastopol in just three months. The first major Russian city in their path was Minsk, which fell in only six days. In order to make clear his determination to win at all costs, Stalin had the three men in charge of the troops defending Minsk executed for their failure to hold their position. This move, along with unspeakable atrocities by the German soldiers against the people of Minsk, solidified the Soviet will. In the future, Russian soldiers would fight to the death rather than surrender, and in July, Stalin exhorted the nation, "It is time to finish retreating. Not one step back! Such should now be our main slogan. ... Henceforth the solid law of discipline for each commander, Red Army soldier, and commissar should be the requirement — not a single step back without order from higher command."

Operation Barbarossa was the most fateful decision of World War II, and when it gave the Soviets common cause with the British (and subsequently the Americans), the purpose of the Lend-Lease Act changed in nature as well. The bulk of Germany's formidable armed forces were committed to the offensive in the east, which relieved the pressure on the British and meant that a German attack on Britain or elsewhere in Western Europe was not going to happen, so keeping the Soviets in the war became the most essential goal of the supply program.

Getting supplies to the Soviets to help them resist the German armies became a strategic imperative, and Iran's geography of bordering the Persian Gulf to the south and Soviet territory to the north brought Iran to the front and center in the strategic supply effort. The German invasion devastated much of European Russia, but also devastated Ukraine and Belarus, other member "republics" in the Soviet Union, and the portions of the Soviet Union that bordered on Iran were Armenia, Azerbaijan and east of the Caspian, Turkmenistan.

During the fighting, the Soviet Union suffered about 25 million killed, with recent estimates placing that huge total even higher. About half of those losses were military, and half civilians. Total German military killed in action or missing in World War II were about 5.2 million, and something like 75-80% of those German military losses were on the Eastern Front. Statistics can be only approximate because of the prolonged chaotic conditions and the immense destruction. The huge area fought over was also the principal arena of the Holocaust, and a literal decimation of the population of Poland.

There were three routes available for sending aid to the Soviet Union. The first route used was the northern route for shipping, which rounded the top of Scandinavia, to the Arctic ports Murmansk and Archangel in the extreme north of the U.S.S.R. This was the shortest route, but it ran a gauntlet of German submarines, surface raiders and aircraft. Convoys assembled from ports in Britain, Canada, and Iceland, and then were shepherded by numerous naval escorts. This route was initially preferred by the Soviets because of proximity to the battlefront, but the loss of ships was heavy.

The second route used in sending aid is little known today. It ran from the U.S. Northwest and Alaska to Vladivostok in the Soviet Far East, on the Sea of Japan. Japan and the Soviet Union were not at war, so Soviet flagged and crewed ships qualified as neutrals and could safely carry cargo very close to Japan. However, the complexities of international law made it prudent to send only food and other non-military by ship, although military aircraft were flown from Alaska to Siberia. This route could have been interrupted at any time by an outbreak of hostilities between Japan and the Soviets, so shipping war materiel was unwise. War did not break out between the two nations until August 1945, when the Red Army attacked Manchuria.

The third and default route was through Iran from the Persian Gulf to the Soviet area of Azerbaijan. It was very rough terrain with a minimal modern infrastructure, and it was many thousands of miles from the U.S., but the German ability to interfere with the route was minimal. This route through Iran came to be called the "Persian Corridor."

The Persian Corridor involved British and Dominion forces, as well as Soviet armed forces and personnel, but the operation and management of the Persian Corridor became largely an American show. Most of the immense amount of aid sent was for transshipment across Iran to the Soviets, but it also involved supplying British and Commonwealth forces in Iran, Iraq and elsewhere in the Middle East. Some was used to feed and supply Iran's people, and some was used to modernize and maintain Iran's infrastructure. There was also the need to supply the American troops working in the Persian Corridor. While 80% or so of the aid came from the U.S., there was also a significant amount of aid sent from Canada, Australia, South Africa and especially India.

The British and Soviets both occupied substantial areas within Iran, but running the Persian Corridor was conducted by Americans. Few American combat troops were involved, and while all the 30,000 Americans soldiers serving in the Persian Corridor had at least some basic combat training, the effort was conducted by U.S. Army service troops who were trained in support, not combat, roles. It's not well-known, but the U.S. Army then had a sizable and very capable Military Railroad Service, an effective Military Transport Service, and a number of specialized engineering units. The core units already existed and were able to quickly expand by incorporating experienced civilians.

These units constructed and managed ports and port facilities, built highways and managed massive trucking systems, built and ran railroads, operated a pipeline and ran huge facilities that assembled trucks, railroad rolling stock and aircraft. They sent an immense amount of aid that substantially helped the Red Army fend off and finally defeat the Germans.

The Strategic Importance of Persia

Persia, the traditional name for Iran, had once been a powerful force in the Middle East, an empire nearly equal to the power of the Romans, Byzantines and Ottoman Turks and the empires in India. For almost 2,000 years, the Persian dynasties had been great military powers, and, culturally, Persian influence spread from Istanbul to Samarkand to Delhi. Middle Easterners wrote poetry in Persian, and Persian art and literature had high status. Persian fashions and manners spread very widely. After Islam was established in Persia, Persian culture profoundly affected the Islamic world.

In more recent centuries, Persian influence and glory was tarnished by military defeat at the hands of the Russians and Turks, and the rise of regional warlords within the country reduced Persia to a ghost of its former power and influence, subject to the whims of the Ottomans, Russians and British. In the 1600s and 1700s, in a series of unequal wars, Tsarist Russia annexed several Persian provinces. The Turkic Qajar dynasty took control of Persia in 1789, and ruled, not very effectively, until 1925. At the turn of the 19th century, Persia, not yet called Iran, was a political backwater until an ocean of oil was discovered in the south of the country around 1908.

During World War I, Iran was utterly powerless to

oppose Russian, British and Ottoman armies fighting each other and crossing into Iranian territory whenever it was convenient for them to do so. Russian troops had occupied some of northern Iran beginning in 1911 after issuing an ultimatum that Iran should observe agreements about Russian rights in Iran - the Russians had invaded northern Iran several times in past centuries and had imposed treaties that favored Russian interests. Russian troops, in the form of the Red Army, did not pull out of Iran until 1921 (Atabaki).

The regional political geography was vastly different then. In 1914, British India included what is now Pakistan, and bordered Iran on the east. The Ottoman empire then controlled what is now Iraq, as well as some of the Arabian areas on the west side of the Persian Gulf. Russia bordered Iran on both sides of the Caspian Sea on Persia's northwest and northeast border. Russia ruled what are now independent Azerbaijan and the Central Asian states, which would become "republics" in the Soviet Union following the Russian Revolution. Persia was surrounded on three sides by predatory empires, and on the south, had a vast resource of oil that attracted the interest of empires.

A vast and important shift in the political geography occurred as a consequence of World War I. The Ottoman empire was destroyed, and Tsarist Russia fell into revolution and chaos, resulting in the creation of the Soviet Union in the early 1920s. The Ottoman Empire was carved up into French-controlled Syria and Lebanon, and British-controlled Jordan, Palestine and Iraq. Iraq became independent in the early 1930s, with Britain retaining large military bases in the country. The Arabian portions of Ottoman territory joined a newly independent Arabia under the new Saudi dynasty. The Anatolian core of the Ottoman empire emerged as Turkey and managed to fight off an invasion by the Greeks and invasion threats by the British, Italians and French.

Oil had been discovered in Iran near the Persian Gulf, and by the outbreak of the war in 1914, the refinery at Abadan on the Gulf coast near the Iraq border was already one of the largest in the world. It became of major strategic significance when the British First Lord of the Admiralty, Winston Churchill, converted the Royal Navy from coal to oil to power the country's ships. Churchill's decision was part of the naval arms race between the British and the Germans in the decade before 1914, one of the rivalries leading to the war.

Churchill during the war

Warships using oil were faster, could get steam up more quickly, and did not have the huge plumes of smoke that gave away the presence of coal-powered naval forces. Oil also powered the new turbine power plants being installed in newly built ships that made warships much faster and more efficient. While Britain had huge reserves of quality coal, there were no oilfields in the British Isles, and the vital oil had to be obtained from Iran.

The Persian oil resources were developed by a commercial entity named the Anglo-Persian Oil Company, known as AIOC. A British venture capitalist named William Knox D'Arcy decided Iran offered the possibility of oil resources. He put together an explorative company and made a deal with the Qajar government for a 60-year lease on any oilfields discovered, in return for a payment of 20,000 pounds sterling, company stock and 16% of any profits. Exploration began, some oil was found in 1905, and an immense deposit was discovered in 1908.

D'Arcy

A refinery was constructed at Abadan on an island, and the refinery quickly became the world's largest. In 1914, the British government by an act of Parliament bought a controlling interest of 53% of the company's shares. It's unclear if it was a forced sale, or if the British managers of the company suggested the deal, but either way, the agreement was close to a British takeover of the company because the agreement allowed the government to appoint two officials who had complete veto power over any company actions. This arrangement effectively made the oil company an unofficial agency of the British government from 1914 onwards.

The company and the British Admiralty cut a sweetheart deal by signing an agreement that AIOC would provide the Royal Navy oil for 30 years, at substantially reduced prices. The agreement did not allow Anglo-Persian to supply other national naval forces. The reduced price for the oil cheated Iran out of substantial royalties.

The company was renamed the Anglo-Iranian Oil Company in the 1930s, when Reza Shah pushed for the name "Iran" to replace "Persia." By 1939, Abadan had a storage capacity of 10 million barrels of oil and had become a huge strategic factor and, by 1939, the Shah's government was dependent on royalties from Anglo-Iranian. The company, under various names, is the ancestor of today's BP (Enc Iranica).

Reza Shah

The oil fields and the Abadan refinery were only a few miles from the Ottoman provinces that made up Iraq. Because of the growing importance of oil as a strategic resource, Britain was concerned that either political disorder in Iran, or an invasion from Ottoman Iran could endanger Abadan. British forces occupied much of southern Iran in 1914, and they too, did not pull out of Iran until 1921.

The British initially moved large numbers of troops from

the Indian Army into southern Iran to protect the oil, but after the Ottomans joined the Germans in 1915, the British occupied Ottoman Basra and moved up the rivers, suffering a military disaster at Kut before eventually occupying Baghdad. The British forces that occupied Iran and conquered Iraq were largely from India and the Commonwealth.

During World War I, there was one German attempt at destroying the Abadan complex. German agents bribed some dissident members of an important clan, who attacked and managed to damage some important pipelines. Overall, the damage was minimal, but the attack reinforced the British sense of vulnerability (Enc Irainca).

With the collapse of Tsarist Russia in 1917, the Russian forces in northeastern Turkey retreated back into the Caucasus. Ottoman forces moved east into the Caucasus, capturing the Azerbaijan oil port and capital of Baku and occupying part of northwestern and northern Iran. They remained there until the war was over.

Iran suffered not only invasion and occupation by three belligerents during World War I, but also severe domestic turmoil. The Qajar dynasty had virtually no power left, and there were regional rebellions of tribal leaders. There was social unrest in the big cities because of food shortages. Most of the country suffered from food shortages, partly caused by the appropriations of the three invading armies, and partly caused by a severe drought. Epidemics broke out, including cholera, and the Spanish flu hit hard. One result was famine, and in 1918-19, the combination of epidemics and starvation is estimated to have killed two million people or more in Iran (Atabaki).

The only Iranian military force in the country was the Iranian Cossack Regiment, a unit with an extremely complicated history. In 1921, one of the Regiment's officers, Reza Khan, used his forces to support a coup against the Qajars and set up a national assembly. The assembly reduced the last Qajar ruler to the status of a puppet, although the national assembly itself did not control much more than the capital, Tehran.

Reza Khan was the force behind the coup, and in 1925 the assembly declared the Qajar dynasty officially over and proclaimed Reza Khan as the new ruler. He took the dynastic name Reza Shah Pahlevi. He proved ruthless and energetic, and he gradually consolidated his control over the country, taming the warlords and quelling disturbances in the cities.

Reza was a military autocrat, but he wanted Iran to be controlled by Iranians. His government was poor, but it did get some income from royalties paid by the Anglo-Iranian Oil Company, and the Iranians used much of it to improve the country's roads and communications. He also invested heavily in roads, as well as building a rail link from the Persian Gulf to Tehran. These links became strategically valuable when war came again, though not necessarily for Iran.

The Allies Occupy Iran

In 1941, after the German invasion of the Soviet Union began, Great Britain and the Soviet Union issued a demand to Iran that the country expel all German nationals and permit the use of the Trans-Iran Railroad to ship supplies from the Gulf to the U.S.S.R. The Shah, who was a proud Persian despite his ruthless leadership, refused the ultimatum. Reza Shah had pushed hard for modernizing Persia, and he is largely responsible for the shift in name of the nation from Persia to Iran, which was intended to emphasize the country's future rather than its past.

In response to the Shah's refusal of the ultimatum, on August 25, 1941, in a military campaign called Operation Countenance, the British and Soviets invaded. British forces advanced into Persia from Iraq and the Gulf, while Soviet forces invaded Persia from both the Caucasus and from Central Asia east of the Caspian Sea. The attack began when the HMS *Shoreham* steamed into Abadan harbor and sank most of the small Iranian navy, killing its commander. The Indian Army's 8th division and elements of the 10th then invaded from newly conquered Iraq and from Kuwait, with support from British tanks and the Royal Air Force. The Soviet 44th, 47th, and 53rd armies invaded from both sides of the Caspian Sea. About 800 Iranian soldiers died in a futile attempt to resist the invasion, while British and Soviet casualties consisted of only a few dozen each. The Iranians sued for peace, which was granted on condition that the Shah abdicate.

HMS *Shoreham*

A picture of a Soviet tank during the campaign

The Allied military intervention was not a complete occupation of Iran. The British forces occupied the oil fields and the Abadan refinery complex, the ports and other strategic places. The Soviets occupied key points in the north of Iran, particularly rail and road centers and ports on the Caspian Sea. They immediately acted to gain control of the Iranian State Railroad.

The two powers divided the country into two zones of influence, with the Soviets predominating in the north and the British in the south. Tehran, the capital, was not occupied, but substantial Soviet forces were stationed nearby. The Shah reluctantly abdicated, and the Allies placed his more compliant son, Mohammed Reza Shah Pahlavi, on the throne. The deposed Shah was exiled to South Africa, where he died a few years later, and Mohammed Reza Pahlavi ruled Iran from then until the Islamic Revolution in the late 1970s. The young Shah was compliant and not yet the fiercely monarchical leader he became in his later years (Zimmerman).

Mohammed Reza Pahlavi

The invading armies negotiated with the new Iranian regime and signed a treaty in January 1942 through which the Allies agreed to withdraw from Iran no later than 6 months after the war ended. The new Shah and his government had little choice but to agree and accept the terms offered.

Shah Reza had invested heavily in developing Iran's infrastructure by investing much of the oil royalties' revenue, but transportation and communication remained primitive in much of Iran. Iran had built a trunk railroad, named the Iran State Railway, from a port on the Persian Gulf to the capital Tehran and points north, opening it in 1939. As it was a potential link between the Gulf and Soviet territory, it increasingly interested both the British and the Soviets as the Germans drove deeper and deeper into Soviet territory.

The British and Russians had both repeatedly interfered in domestic Persian affairs, and both, as well as the Ottoman Turks, had invaded Persia during World War I. The British had virtually controlled the region around the massive Abadan refinery between two wars, assuring that it remained in British hands, and retaining control of Abadan became a major concern for the British after World War II began in 1939. Actual Iranian sovereignty was not something that much concerned either the British or the Soviets.

Earlier in 1941, the British had invaded Iraq, but an Iraqi military commander named Rashid Ali conducted a coup, ousting the pro-British ruler, Prince Abdul Ilah, and taking power himself. Rashid Ali was interested in obtaining German support as a way to counter British dominance in Iraq, and he wanted to get rid of the notable British bases in his country. The British saw him as dangerously pro-German. France had been defeated by the Germans in June 1940, and the French Vichy collaborationist government ruled in the French colonies of Lebanon and Syria. In theory, the Vichy regime and a pro-German Iraq gave the Germans a route to interfere with Iran or even attack the vital Iranian oilfields.

The British demanded that Rashid Ali step down, and when he refused, the British invaded. There was a short but sharp British-Iraqi war from May 2-31, and during the campaign, there was a small intervention from Italy and Germany in the form of a few aircraft attacking British positions from bases in Vichy Syria. Ultimately, the German and Italian air attacks had little impact, and the British quickly won, using troops largely from India. After that, they returned Abdul Ilah to nominal rule in Iraq (Johnson).

In May 1941, German attacks on the oilfields in Iran briefly seemed to be a real possibility. The notorious German Afrika Korps, under its legendary commander Erwin Rommel, appeared in Africa in February 1941, originally assigned to help Italy fight the British in the Italian North African colony of Libya. Rommel inflicted severe defeats on British forces, and a German push into Egypt to seize the Suez Canal was greatly feared. The Afrika Korps was pushed back from the borders of Egypt, but it remained a threat until the Allied invasion of North Africa in 1943 eliminated German forces there.

Meanwhile, the British solved the threat of German and Italian forces based in the Vichy colonies by invading Syria and Lebanon, and eventually assisting the anti-German Free French to take control of both of the colonies.

The Persian Corridor

By 1940, Britain was near bankruptcy, and feeding and defending Britain itself was becoming increasingly difficult. Britain's lifeline for food and military supplies depended on convoys crossing the Atlantic from Canada and the United States, and though not yet at war, the U.S. had cautiously joined the British in defending shipping convoys from German submarines. The British had allowed American naval forces to use British and imperial bases in exchange for 50 old destroyers, so close military cooperation began well before either Lend-Lease or American declarations of war. A stubborn Congress allowed the British to obtain American products, provided they were paid for and preferably carried in British shipping.

The genesis of Lend-Lease was a letter that Prime Minister Churchill sent in December 1940 to President Roosevelt, explaining that Britain was close to bankruptcy and would soon no longer be able to pay for American food and military supplies. Congress had been leery of involvement in the war and passed a number of neutrality acts designed to prevent the president from acting to commit the U.S. to any involvement in the war, but Roosevelt feared a British collapse and what that might mean for the United States. All the while, Roosevelt had a very difficult time overcoming American isolationist sentiment. He finally managed to convince Congress to pass legislation titled "An Act to Further the Defense of the United States," allowing transfer of weapons and other resources to the British. It became better known as "Lend-Lease," as phrasing it as a way of defending the country helped it become more popular with the public (Johnson).

The Lend-Lease legislation was signed by Roosevelt in March 1941, and the initial focus was on aiding Britain since the Germans had not yet attacked the Soviets. Roosevelt famously described it as lending a garden hose to a neighbor whose house was on fire, a bit of simple rhetoric that seems to have had a profound impact on public attitudes. The name "Lend-Lease" was also extremely effective at overcoming opposition because it implied that what was lent would be returned when it was no longer needed, which quieted members of Congress opposed to simply giving Britain aid with no conditions attached.

A picture of Roosevelt signing the bill

The Lend-Lease legislation placed a great deal of power in the president's hands, and he could simply declare countries to be eligible for Lend-Lease. President Roosevelt used his powers under the Act to add countries to those eligible for the Lend-Lease program, among them China, Australia, New Zealand and eventually the Soviet Union, which immediately made the Persian Corridor a matter of strategic significance. The materials sent to the Soviets and the other nations through the program included a vast quantity and range of goods, from fighter aircraft and railroad locomotives, to chocolate bars and field telephones, cigarettes, copper and steel, and millions of pairs of boots.

Easily overlooked in the complicated geopolitics of the time is that shortly before World War II started, the Germans and Soviets had secretly signed a non-aggression pact. The British despised the Nazis, but they were also wary of the Soviets as a threat to the Iranian oilfields, and Soviets opposed the British invasion of Iraq. This situation was turned upside down when the Germans invaded the Soviet Union in June 1941, initially inflicting severe defeats on the Soviet armies. Suddenly, Iran was sandwiched between two allies and formed a possible link between them. This became critical as the German armies pushed ever deeper into the U.S.S.R.

The Soviets immediately requested help from Britain and the United States. The U.S. was not officially at war until December 1941, six months after the German invasion began, but soon after the German attack began, President Roosevelt added the Soviet Union to the Lend-Lease program. Initially, the Soviets strongly preferred for supplies to be delivered by shipping that sailed north of Norway to the Arctic ports of Murmansk and Archangel because the ports were closer to the battle front. The British did not have the ability to fully develop the Persian

Corridor and the Americans were initially skeptical, but the increasing number of ships sunk on the Northern route generated further interest in Iran (Coakley 238).

An accumulation of crises forced the use of the Iran route. The German offensives pushed into the northern Caucasus and the Africa Korps pushed into Egypt, rousing fears of a German offensive that would cut off the Suez Canal and even threaten the Abadan refinery complex. German domination of the Mediterranean closed off the Black Sea as a possible supply route (Coakley 238).

The Persian Corridor route soon supplanted the Northern route. The German occupation of Norway meant that the convoys faced a gauntlet of German submarines, surface naval raiders. and Luftwaffe planes the whole way there and the whole way back, inflicting unacceptable losses. The Arctic ports were also difficult to operate in winter when icy conditions and very rough weather affected the ports, and when rough seas made the voyages to the ports difficult.

In the summer of 1942, a large convoy designated PQ-17 headed for the Soviet Arctic ports. PQ-17 had an impressive naval escort, but the Germans went all out, attacking with planes, submarines, and other ships, destroying 24 of the 35 ships in the convoy. The loss of 24 ships meant the loss of the large amounts of aid they carried, and a heavy loss of life among the crews. At that point in the war, German submarines were sinking far more merchant ships than were being built, resulting in a severe shortage of shipping to carry aid to Britain, let alone to the U.S.S.R.

German occupation of most of Europe and the domination of the Mediterranean made the route to the Soviet Union through the Black Sea impossible. The situation only changed late in 1944 when the Germans had been driven out of North Africa, Italy had surrendered, and the Black Sea region had largely been cleared of Axis forces. The Mediterranean was much less dangerous by the end of 1944, and the route through the Dardanelles began to be used, but from 1941-1944, the Persian Corridor was extremely important as the main channel to get weapons to the Red Army.

A third route was from the United States and Canada to Vladivostok on the Sea of Japan. Japan and the Soviets were not at war, so Soviet-flagged ships could carry Lend-Lease close to northern Japan, although this route was not used much for war material. A part of this route also consisted of flying aircraft from Alaska to Siberia across the Bering Strait, well north of Japan, where Japanese air cover was weak or non-existent. The aircraft were piloted by Soviet pilots and the ships were manned by Soviet crews, so they were technically neutral. International law was ambivalent about neutral shipping and transporting war material, and since the very large amount of aid traveling the route was not war material, the Japanese did not interfere with the route. Supplies shipped to Vladivostok also had thousands of miles to go along the Trans-Siberian railway before they reached European Soviet territory.

Since the Northern route was so dangerous and the U.S. West Coast to Vladivostok shipping route was tacitly used only for food and support for the civilian population, the remaining possible route became obvious: from the Persian Gulf north through Iran to the Soviet Union. There was no danger of the German military affecting the route, even as the environment in Iran posed considerable difficulty for transport. Shipping from Canada and the United States sailed to the region via very long voyages, either from the U.S. and Canada across the Pacific and then north through the Indian Ocean, or from the U.S. and Canada east around Africa via Africa's Cape of Good Hope to the Indian Ocean and then north. The route for shipping from the West Coast to the Persian Gulf ports was 18,000 miles and 14,000 miles from the East Coast. The route took a ship up to several months, but few ships were actually lost. Several ships intended to sail for the Persian Corridor were sunk by German submarines in the Caribbean, but by and large, the supply route was secure.

There was some danger from German and Japanese submarines, but the fate of PQ-17 made clear the need for the Persian route, and in September, Roosevelt declared the creation of the U.S. Military Iranian Mission. In 1942, it was renamed the Persian Gulf Service Command, the PGSC, with a mission that covered Iran, Iraq, and the parts of Arabia adjacent to the Persian Gulf.

At this time, the U.S. was very poorly prepared for any involvement in the Middle East. The U.S. War Department was so completely unprepared that it had no maps of the region. The State Department Division of Near Eastern Affairs had a staff of 13, and a total of three people who could speak one or two of the many regional languages (Johnson).

As a result, the British began the transfer of Lend-Lease and other support to the Soviets before the Americans arrived in Iran in force. They shipped 41,000 tons to the Soviet Union in September 1942, peaking at 51,000 tons in January 1943. The British shipped their own kinds of aid, separate from Lend-Lease but with the same goals, and also shipped American Lend-Lease aid. When American aid began to flood in and Americans took over the management of the Persian Corridor, there was a sharp increase in the amount of aid reaching the Soviets, up to 101,000 tons in April 1943 and 199,000 tons by that September, as the road and railroad systems were enhanced. The peak delivery was 282,097 long tons delivered to the Soviet Union in July 1944 (Coakley 251-52).

Aircraft, railway locomotives, railway rolling stock, machinery and trucks sent from the United States to the Persian Corridor were broken down and crated before shipment, and had to be assembled after unloading cargo in Iran. The U.S. Army set up two truck assembly plants, one in Khorramshahr and the other in Andimeshk, which, together, eventually employed thousands of Iranian civilians. Khorramshahr is a port, so assembly took place not far from where the cargo was unloaded. Andimeshk is a hundred or so miles into the interior, so the aircraft, trucks and other material was shipped to the assembly plant by rail. There was an aircraft assembly plant at Abadan. The Military Railroad Service set up locations where locomotives and boxcars could be assembled (Smith).

Getting equipment to the Soviets required several large-scale infrastructure projects. The first was to rebuild the port facilities at Khorramshahr to make it an effective deep water port that could dock and unload ships quickly. The second was construction of the aircraft assembly plant at Abadan, which was begun by the British and turned into a large scale facility by the Americans. The third was the construction of the truck assembly plant in the interior transportation center of Andimeshk. There was, for a time, a barge assembly site, just inside the Iraq border, through which American assemblers put together some 300 barges, which were then turned over to the British for use on the river routes to Baghdad and points north in Iraq (Johnson).

During the war, the aircraft assembly plant in Iran assembled almost 5,000 planes, including the P-39, P-40, P-47, P-63, B-25 and AT-6 aircraft, which were primarily varieties of fighter aircraft and some medium bombers. The assembled planes were inspected, tested, had the red star insignia painted on and were either flown to Soviet-controlled airfields in northern Iran, where Soviet pilots flew them to the U.S.S.R., or flown directly from the plant by Soviet pilots. Many of them went directly into combat. The truck assembly plant assembled almost 200,000 trucks, particularly the Studebaker trucks. The trucks were loaded with Lend-Lease cargo and driven to Soviet-controlled points in the north, inspected and then turned over to Soviet drivers for the run into the Soviet Union (Johnson).

Overall, of the millions of tons of materials sent to the Soviets by the Lend-Lease program, about half traveled via the route from the U.S. West Coast to Vladivostok in Siberia, a quarter via the Persian Corridor and most of the rest by the Northern route to Murmansk. The Persian route was particularly important in providing weapons (Wynn).

The war began in September 1939 with the German attack on Poland, with the Soviets actually being German allies until the German attack on the U.S.S.R. in June 1941. The British had maintained strong military forces in the region even before the war began, to defend the vital Abadan refinery and to guard the sea lanes for oil tankers.

The German entry into the war in North Africa made supplying the British forces in Egypt and those fighting the Afrika Korps by convoy across the Mediterranean very dangerous. Supplies from South Africa and Australia, New Zealand, particularly from India, and from other Dominion regions could ship through the Red Sea and through Suez, and American aid could ship across the Pacific or around Africa's Cape of Good Hope. These routes supplied the British army in Egypt and North Africa. British forces could also be supplied via the Persian Gulf and through Iraq.

When the British invaded Iraq in May 1941 and southern Iran in September, conditions changed. A compliant Iraq allowed shipment up the Persian Gulf and through Iraq, and with the Soviet armies reeling, shipping arms and supplies through Iran began immediately after the occupation of Iran, and the British began working to improve the port, rail and road infrastructure. The immediate British aid probably helped Soviet resistance, but to what extent is unknown. The capacity of Iran's system before the British invasion was only 6,000 long tons a month, not even a single shipload (Coakley 229).

The British technical services managed to get the Iranian system modernized enough to supply about 70,000 long tons in a month, but they simply did not have the resources to develop it much further. They also had to continue supplying their own 8th Army fighting Rommel's forces, and the largely Indian 10th Army occupying Iraq (Oakley 230).

Iranian oil and gasoline from Abadan fueled most of the trucks and aircraft, as well as shipping. It produced a great deal of aviation gasoline exported to the Soviet Union. It literally fueled the Persian Corridor, and meant that oil tankers from the U.S. and the Americas did not need to supply fuel the way they did in other theaters of operation. The primary Iran resources were the oil and geography.

The British had already begun sending aid to the Soviets, but simply did not have the resources to improve the rail and road infrastructure to the extent needed. After American involvement began, the British and Americans divided functions along the Persian Corridor, with the British responsible for security and the Americans responsible for managing road, railroad and other transportation infrastructure. The Soviets were to receive shipments in northern Iran and move them along into the U.S.S.R. proper. The Soviets did not want British or American drivers or pilots to enter the U.S.S.R. (Zimmerman).

German military threats to the Persian Corridor were minimal, at least once their offensive drive into the Caucasus was finally stopped. They were never close to Iran or to the Soviet oil fields in Baku in Azerbaijan, though there was still a threat from German special operations and from a few spies. The British were generally responsible for security in the south of Iran, although American-run routes and facilities also had security forces, both to keep order and to watch for sabotage.

In 1941, there were about 2,000 German nationals in Iran. Some were diplomatic personnel, some worked with German-owned businesses, and a few seem to have been German military or secret service operatives. When the Allies invaded Iran, one demand was that Iran expel all German nationals. There were several German merchant ships in Abadan harbor, which were taken over and sent to India. One German crew scuttled their ship. German women and children were repatriated to Germany via Turkey, and German diplomats were interned in Australia

(O'Sullivan 42-45).

The U.S. Army

Delivering the immense amount of Lend-Lease materials destined for the Eastern Front that were sent through the Persian Corridor was a strategic necessity. The U.S. Army became a formidable fighting machine during the war, but a major portion of the Army's accomplishments were more of the Quartermaster and supply kind than combat. Lend-Lease aid sent by the Northern route involved the Merchant Marine, and aid sent to Vladivostok from the U.S. Pacific Northwest and Alaska involved civilian-controlled ports and Soviet ships and aircrews. In the Persian Corridor, the U.S. Army was literally the prime mover, and various uniformed service units built and ran ports, a thousand-mile trucking route, and an entire nation's railroads.

The U.S. Army Port Service took control of the port at Khorramshahr in December 1942 and ran it until July 1945. Just as the Army had truck and train units, it also had port units. The 378th, 380th and 482nd Port Battalions arrived and began operations in this and other ports, and the personnel involved included longshoremen, cargo checkers, warehouse foremen, crane operators and others. Eventually, Iranian employees were trained to do these specialized tasks, but that took time (Bykofsky 395).

Improving the port meant building docks and equipping them with cranes, building warehouses and managing them, controlling ship traffic in the port, controlling the unloading of ships and tracking what was supposed to go where, and guarding against theft and potential sabotage. It also meant finding skilled port managers and finding people in the Army with experience as longshoremen. At first, the time it took for unloading cargo was quite slow, but things improved a great deal as the ports were developed (Johnson). Bringing them up to the level that the flow of Lend-Lease required meant shipping in heavy equipment from the U.S., including cranes and other equipment for unloading ships. All this took time and accounts for why it took several months from the start of the American efforts in the Persian Corridor to hit the 100,000 tons per month level. In the summer of 1945, the port assets were turned over to the British by the departing American service units, and the British eventually turned the assets over to the Iranians.

The refinery at Abadan was a British project, but Americans helped develop the port at the city. They built and operated a 155-mile-long pipeline to the truck assembly point at Andimeshk. Building a pipeline meant that both the piping and the construction equipment needed to build it had to be imported (Johnson).

The Abadan refinery was also involved in a sort of

reverse Lend-Lease. About 500,000 tons of aviation fuel from the refinery was shipped to the Soviets via tanker rail cars, and the amount was "replaced" by shipping an equivalent amount of American aviation fuel to Britain (Motter 306).

The Army already had a Motor Transport Service, composed of specialists in trucks, which proved to be extraordinarily important in supplying Allied troops in the campaigns in North Africa, Italy, and the campaign in Western Europe after Normandy. Unlike those places, trucking in the Persian Corridor faced little danger from enemy action. There was no need for anti-aircraft guns or armored vehicles protecting truck convoys. The main was the wear and tear brought about by occasionally extreme environmental conditions.

The Military Transport Service had difficulty obtaining experienced truck drivers, as they were considered essential to the American economy and were deferred from the military draft. The War Department worked with the Teamsters Union and trucking companies, and it advertised the need for volunteer truckers for a "secret mission." More than a thousand drivers gave up their draft deferments and joined up to drive a variety of trucks, including semis, 10-ton Mack trucks, and standard 6 x 4s. In all, the truckers stationed in Iran drove an estimated 97 million miles in Lend-Lease missions (Johnson).

The British controlled southern Iran, and their rules were
not always helpful. Initially, the Americans had difficulty
hiring and maintaining Iranian workers and crews because
the British-imposed wage scale was set very low. The
British vetoed letting the Americans pay higher rates,
which initially stymied attempts to obtain sufficient
Iranian labor. Without Iranian labor, running the system
would have been nearly impossible (Motter).

Food was in short supply in Iran, and millions of Iranians
and their families were going hungry. The Americans
came up with a program of certificates redeemable for
food, sugar, bread, tea, and other necessities that
supplemented pay, which had strong appeal.
Implementing the program resulted in the easier
recruitment of qualified or trainable Iranian workers, and
much better motivation for Iranian employees (Weital).

The Military Transport Service in Iran had about 2,000
trucks at any one time, engaged in carrying cargo from the
ports to points where they were unloaded and turned over
to the Soviets for shipment. This was separate from the
trucks assembled and designated for shipment to the
U.S.S.R., which also carried Lend-Lease cargo. Those
trucks switched to Soviet drivers and continued on into
the U.S.S.R. with whatever cargo they carried.

Most American trucks were not designed for the rigorous

conditions of trucking in Iran simply because they were designed for the good roads and milder environment of the U.S. Most trucks used by the MTS in Iran were good for only about 50,000 miles before they were no longer worth the effort to repair them. The Mack Truck diesels were typically serviceable for about 100,000 miles (Motter 326).

In the beginning, the MTS also had severe problems with accidents, some of them caused by reckless driving by inexperienced drivers. Safety was improved by establishing repair and service points, and by awards for safe driving. Truckers with exemplary records were rewarded with leave and trips to the Holy Land, via truck to Basra, by rail from Basra to Baghdad, and then on to Palestine by truck. Hundreds of drivers took advantage of the program (Johnson).

In September 1943, soldier drivers had an accident rate of 22.2 per million truck miles, and native drivers had a rate of 189.9 accidents per million truck miles. Better training and recognition of good safety records reduced the rate to 6.7 accidents per million by late 1944 (Bykofsky 422). Drivers with exemplary safety records were rewarded, but there was also a system of publicly identifying units with less enviable records. Each month, the trucking unit with the worst safety record was presented with a white elephant emblem (Motter 324).

Efficient trucking required a major upgrading of roads in Iran. This included grading, widening the roads and eventually asphalting them. The 636-mile main road between Khorramshahr and Kazvin was a 2-lane gravel highway. All but 50 miles of this road had been asphalted by the end of 1943 and all of it by 1944. These were not four-lane superhighways, but they were equivalent to two-lane paved American roads and were probably the best in the Middle East.

The heavy truck traffic meant that roads required constant maintenance. Roads were, depending on the section of the road and the season, subject to intense heat, subzero temperatures, flooding, snowdrifts, rockslides, avalanches, and sometimes theft. The Quartermaster Truck units established relay, repair, and service units at regular intervals along the main route. Radio and field telephones allowed truck convoys to keep in constant touch with other units and to summon emergency aid if needed (Bykofsky 415-16).

The Transport Service had to develop not just a large cadre of drivers, but recruit and train Iranians as laborers, service technicians, and drivers. It also required developing communications along the entire route, including radio facilities, teletype, and field telephone services, which meant stringing and maintaining thousands of miles of wire. As such, copper wire was a highly valued commodity on the black market, so theft was a continuing problem (Johnson).

One crucially important element to getting Lend-Lease to the Soviet Union is virtually unknown to most Americans: The Military Railroad Service, known as the MRS. The U.S. Army had first become involved in railroading during the Civil War and had maintained some units concerned with the military use of railroads since that time. In World War II, the MRS ran thousands of miles of rail services in most of the places where U.S. troops went, except for the Pacific islands. The MRS quickly built and ran railroads to supply American and Allied armies in North Africa, Sicily, Italy, and France. (Newel 7).

The already existing military service units were expanded and more of them formed. A typical example is that in June 1941, the Army organized the 711th Railroad Operating Battalion. The unit was given basic military training, but their focus was on operating railways in the context of supplying military units. The 711th's training included actually building a railway between two Army bases in Louisiana. To make the training more realistic, the 25 railroad bridges along the route were periodically blown up. Many of the officers and men assigned to these service battalions had experience in running American railroads. Units formed later went through similar training

(Army History).

A unique railroading program called the "Affiliation Plan" was developed before the war by the U.S. Army Corps of Engineers. Through this plan, American railroad lines would affiliate with a specific MRS unit. The railroads would designate personnel, who, if they passed a physical, would be given some military training and then be appointed officers in the Army Reserve. Then if war came, they would be assigned as officers to the MRS unit their railroad was sponsored. This assured a cadre of experienced railroad operators in all of the military railroad construction and maintenance units. It seems to have worked quite well during the war when the MRS ran many thousands of miles of track on three continents, using 33 MRS railway operating battalions and 11 railway shop battalions (Newel 8).

The Army railroad units were capable of quickly organizing rail support. Unlike civilian rail operations, the units were also trained to destroy the railway infrastructure, in case of an enemy offensive, although there was no incident of that in the Persian Corridor. The formal organization of a railroad battalion was a headquarters company, and three or four lettered companies with specific duties assigned to them.

The headquarters company scheduled and dispatched

trains, kept track of supplies and was responsible for signals and communications. Company A maintained and repaired track, switches, water tanks and other structures. Company B operated the roundhouse, and maintained the rolling stock, with one platoon responsible for locomotives and the other for boxcars. Company C had teams to operate trains, yards and stations (Army History).

This degree of formal organization was typical, not just of the Military Railroad Service, but also for trucking units, construction engineer battalions, port operations battalions and the others kinds of military support units. In remote Iran, the formal structures were maintained, but soldiers did what was necessary to keep the system working, and American troops seem to have been able to handle the many unexpected situations arising in Iran.

During the war, these Army service units in the Persian Corridor did their work well, after a slow and somewhat tentative start. They operated and maintained railways behind the front lines almost everywhere American combat troops went. Several of the battalions were stationed in Iran and were vital to the efficient movement of immense amounts of material to the Soviet Union. A significant difference in the Iran situation is that the MRT units were not operating close to actual combat zones (Army History).

Iran's state railway was a single-track standard gauge trunk line, and was generally well engineered and solidly built, but its capacity was small, far less than would be needed for the massive flood of Lend-Lease that would eventually arrive. The Iranian line had far too few locomotives and far too little rolling stock. The MRS needed to import large quantities of everything from the United States, including rails, locomotives, signals equipment, boxcars and thousands of experience railroaders. MRS set up shops to assemble locomotives and boxcars. Many of the locomotives were powerful ALCO RSD-1 diesel-electric machines made in Schenectady, New York (Smith).

Harvey Henkelmann's picture of an ALCO RSD-1

The completed Iran State Railway was actually a considerable feat of engineering, requiring workers to bore 131 tunnels across the 165-mile stretch through the rugged Zagros Mountains. However, its capacity was only a few thousand tons per month, far below the needs of the massive Lend-Lease program envisioned. The U.S. Military Railroad Service rebuilt the line and took over management of the Iran State Railroad as far as Tehran and Tabriz, where Soviet railroaders took over, controlling the routes to Azerbaijan and to Central Asia (Johnson). The Iranian railway originally connected Bandar Shapur on the Gulf to Bandar Shah on the Caspian, some 865 miles. A connecting line ran to the city of Tabriz in Iran's northwest, the main transfer point where Soviet operators took over.

In the Persian Corridor, significant MRS operations did not really begin until January 1943. That's when the 711th arrived in Iran. Eventually, other MRS battalions joined them in improving and operating the rail elements of the Persian Corridor. They included the 730th MRS battalion, affiliated with the Pennsylvania Railroad, the 754th which was affiliated with the Southern Pacific Railroad, and the 702nd Railroad Division, a supervisory and management battalion, associated with the Union Pacific. Another unit was formed from drafting personnel from existing MRS battalions and adding soldiers with some railroad experience (Newel 9).

By the fall 1944, the Soviets had pushed the Germans far to the west. The Afrika Korps had been defeated in North

Africa, Italy had surrendered, and German military capability in the Mediterranean and Black Sea had become minimal. This meant that cargo could be shipped through the Mediterranean and to Soviet Black Sea ports, a much shorter route. As a result, the truck assembly plant ceased operations in November 1944 and the aircraft assembly plant shut down operations in December. The assembly plant in Andimeshk was broken down and shipped by rail to the Soviets (Smith).

For some of its existence, the whole mission was considered secret, so soldiers and contracted civilians had their mail heavily censored so as not to reveal possibly compromising information about where they were working, or what they were doing. This required creating another service bureaucracy to run the censorship, because the number of Americans in the Persian Corridor eventually numbered 30,000 military members and thousands of civilian employees, as well as Merchant Marine sailors in the ports and the thousands of Iranian employees (Johnson).

The Americans did their best to assure that the various clan and tribal chiefs were friendly or at least neutral. The clan chiefs' considerable powers could affect the routes north. Paying these powerful leaders a nominal sum and providing them with some weapons ensured a friendly relationship and some protection. There was almost no trouble with these regional leaders (Weital).

Making the Persian Corridor an effective route to the Soviets took a considerable amount of both time and engineering. Iran's physical environment posed real challenges, including 175 miles through the salt desert north of the Persian Gulf ports, where temperatures could reach well above 130 degrees Fahrenheit in the summer, and where blinding and engine-killing sandstorms could occur. A significant part of the route crossed mountains, some as high as 13,000 feet, with hundreds of hair pin turns, a number of very steep grades, and deep snowdrifts during the winter. This was tough for the trucks and drivers alike (Schubert).

The desert portions of the routes north could become so hot that heat exhaustion affected drivers and railroad crews. In early 1943, unexpected heavy rain resulted in floods that destroyed a number of bridges and washed out substantial sections of road. Constant attention was required to keep all the links running smoothly. At its peak, the system required 30,000 Americans, almost all service rather than combat troops, and 43,000 Iranian employees (Motter 239-40).

Sometimes, outside factors had an effect. Early in the Persian Corridor's operation, at least one shipload of heavy equipment needed for roadbuilding was sunk off

Trinidad by a German submarine, delaying some construction (Motter 103).

The U.S. Army established a trucking route from Khorramshahr to Kazvin. Khorramshahr is a port city on the Iranian side of the Shatt al-Arab, the river formed in Iraq when the Tigris and Euphrates rivers merge and flow to the Persian Gulf. Kazvin (now Qazvin) is a city in northern Iran, near the Caspian Sea. From there, material could be trucked on into Azerbaijan in the U.S.S.R. or taken to the Caspian to be loaded on shipping, after cargo was unloaded and taken over by Soviet operations.

Among the differences between Iran and other theaters of operation was building supplies. Iran lacked significant forest resources, so wood for construction had to be imported, much of the little wood available coming from India. In most regions, the U.S. Army built temporary structures, but, in Iran, adobe and kiln bricks were readily available and cheap, and wood was not, so buildings tended to be built from brick. In the arid regions of the south of Iran, the Army experienced some problems with roofing, because the tarpaper over boards salvaged from shipping cases proved unusable. A sand-asphalt material was developed that worked well in the heat and occasional torrential rains. Most of the plumbing and electric fixtures used were imported from the U.S. (Motter 249).

One of the first units arriving in Iran was the 114th Quartermaster Battalion Mobile, an African American trucking supply outfit. They hauled cargo over the 1,000-mile route from Khorramshahr. These members and other units faced a number of significant health issues, including heat exhaustion, malaria, dysentery, an ailment called "sand fly fever," and other problems. The rudimentary medical system prevailing in rural Iran was incapable of dealing with changed conditions and had to be replaced by the construction of modern facilities appropriately staffed in order to care for the influx of tens of thousands of Americans. In the same vein, rations were at first haphazard, and soldiers supplemented them by shooting wild boars and gazelles (Barni and Long 2).

At the time, the U.S. Army was then rigidly segregated, so black soldiers were concentrated in service rather than combat units. Segregation of African American units was a characteristic of anywhere American troops were stationed in World War II, but in some of the more remote areas, fraternization with the locals occurred and segregation was somewhat relaxed. Black Army units assigned to the Persian Corridor included the 435th Engineer Dump Truck Company, Company B of the 611th Quartermaster Bakery Battalion, and the 352nd Engineer Regiment. The 352nd regimental band was apparently widely appreciated. About 5,000 of the service troops in the Persian Corridor were African Americans (Motter 244-45).

While drivers could come down with exhaustion, disease, or heat stroke, more than 3,000 trucks were damaged beyond repair from 1943-1945. The almost complete absence of repair and support for motor vehicles also had to be supplemented by the development of effective support. Truckers developed a block relay system in which every 200 miles trucks were serviced and new road crews assigned (Barni and Long, 22).

Communications in most of Iran were minimal, and the Army had to quickly supply ways for truck convoys and trains to keep in contact with their base, and to conduct traffic with maximum efficiency. The 95th Special Service Battalion and other communication specialist units at their peak operated 11 radio stations, 15 teletype stations, 17 field telephone switchboards of 40 to 50 lines each, 500 miles of pole lines, and 8,000 miles of strung wire (Motter 253).

Perhaps not surprisingly, some of the problems never completely solved were corruption and theft. Copper wire was particularly appreciated in the local black markets, and an estimated 250 miles of wire was stolen, causing problems in communication. There was some stealing on the part of employees, but the long lines of communication were vulnerable. Trucks going slow up very steep grades were vulnerable to men jumping onto the backs of trucks and slitting the canvas tarpaulins, reaching in, and tossing cargo to the sides of the road. Railroad box cars also had vulnerable points.

There was also some trouble with ID cards stolen from Iranian employees, forged IDs, forged or stolen time cards, and other petty crimes. That said, the estimate is that theft and accidents cost less than half of one percent of the total of supplies shipped (Motter 324).

The oil facilities around Abadan were defended, but they were vulnerable to sabotage. The British had implemented a plan to completely destroy the refinery and the oil wells if the German forces had managed to break into the Middle East past Suez. One vulnerability was to German or Italian aircraft operating from Iraqi or airfields in Syria controlled by the Vichy regime. The threat from Iraq was eliminated when the British invaded and occupied the country, deposing the pro-German dictator. The threat from Vichy-ruled Syria was solved by invading and occupying Syria and Lebanon (O'Sullivan 129-30).

Several Italian bombers did manage to reach as far as the oil production facilities in Bahrain on the western side of the Persian Gulf, where they inflicted minor damage during one attack. The bombers took off from Italian-occupied territory in Europe, bombed Bahrain, and continued on to the Italian East African colony of Eritrea. The Italians had few air or naval assets in their East African colonies of Eritrea and Somalia, a mild threat which was quickly eliminated by the British. The British subsequently and occupied the Italian colonies during the early stages of the war.

The Germans did not have many long-range aircraft, but a few were capable of reaching Iran from German positions in Russia by flying at high altitude over Turkish airspace. There were several actions in which German operatives were landed in or parachuted into Iran. At least one mission flew at an altitude so high that the agents parachuted into Iran were terrified of the jump and lost all of their equipment. Not much is known about these German operations, except that they had no success. Some of the operations may have been fake, used to create an impression of their capability of long-distance exploits (O'Sullivan 182-83).

Near the end of the war, there was a bizarre German plan to send a crew aboard a trawler around Africa to the Persian Gulf in hopes of damaging Allied shipping and damaging the Abadan refinery. The German trawler was disguised as a Norwegian fishing trawler, the crew could speak Norwegian, and most of the small crew were trained frogmen. The mission was last heard from in a radio message off West Africa, after which the trawler vanished. How a Norwegian fishing trawler in the Persian Gulf would not have attracted curiosity remains unexplained (O'Sullivan 168-69).

The war in Europe ended in May 1945, and the British and American operations in the Persian Corridor began to end what was left of the operations in early 1945. President Truman sharply cut aid to the Soviet Union at the war's official end, precipitating an angry Soviet response. Although the war was finished, the U.S.S.R. had suffered immense damage and wanted Lend-Lease aid in the form of food and industrial resources to continue.

The Soviet forces that invaded the north of Iran in 1941 had numbered about 40,000, but during the war, the number of Soviet troops grew to 100,000. The Soviet armies were slow to leave Iran and did so only under international pressure. In December 1945, the Soviets set up two ostensibly independent republics, including the Autonomous People's Republic of Azerbaijan, which was carved from Iran's northwest, not from the Soviet republic of Azerbaijan. The other was the Kurdish People's Republic. They had recruited thousands of Iranians to form an Iranian communist party in the hope of creating new Soviet satellites. Under prodding by the new United Nations, the Soviets finally left Iran in February 1946, and the Shah's forces promptly invaded and suppressed the two Soviet puppet states (Military History "Gulf").

The Persian Corridor's Impact

A completely unanticipated impact of the Persian Corridor is that it provided an escape route for a large number of Polish refugees. When Germany invaded Poland in September 1939, the Soviets had invaded Poland from the east, with each power taking over about half of Poland. During their occupation of eastern Poland, the Soviets deported well over a million Poles who were considered "socially dangerous" to Central Asia and Siberia, and they eventually murdered tens of thousands of them, with the massacre at the Katyn Forest being the most notorious and thoroughly documented.

There was a Polish government in exile in Britain, which was recognized by the Americans and British but not by the Soviets, who formed their own puppet Polish communist government within the U.S.S.R. When the Germans attacked in June 1941, the head of the Polish government in exile in Britain, Wladyslaw Sikorski, and the Soviet ambassador to Britain, Ivan Mayski, negotiated an agreement allowing Polish refugees to leave the U.S.S.R. via the Persian Corridor. The object was to establish a Polish army in Britain which could then be used when the Allies opened a second front in Europe. The army was headed by General Wladyslaw Anders,

who was released from the Lubyanka prison in Moscow
and allowed to leave by the Persian Corridor. The force
became known as the Anders Army (Holocaust Museum).

Sikorski

   Starting in 1942, Polish refugees began arriving in Iran,
with most arriving in the Caspian Sea port of Pahlavi.
About 74,000 Polish veterans and men of military age
came through Iran as refugees, as did an additional 41,000
civilians, including thousands of orphaned children. Some
5,000-6,000 were Jewish. Many of them arrived in poor
condition, and they were quarantined for a time before

being sent on to Tehran.

Some refugees were forced to stay in Iran, so they set up small community schools that taught in Polish. A few became Iranian citizens. Polish refugees scattered all over the world, with some settling in Kenya, some in what is now Tanzania, some in Britain, some in South Africa, and others in Uganda and Mexico. The Jewish refugees primarily settled in Palestine (Holocaust Museum). All told, estimates of Polish veterans and civilians filtering through Iran are as high as 300,000 (Faruqi).

While there is no way to measure specific impacts, the trucks and jeeps provided to the Soviet armies were particularly significant. In total, the U.S. sent more than 400,000 4-wheel drive vehicles to the U.S.S.R., with tens of thousands more provided by Britain and Canada, about twice as many trucks as the Soviet wartime production of 265,000. The Lend-Lease trucks also appear to have been generally of a higher quality and more robust in the very difficult combat conditions on the Eastern Front. The American vehicles, particularly the Studebaker trucks, were important in providing the Red Army with mobility, and about 20,000 of the Studebaker trucks were modified into carrying the deadly Katyusha rocket launchers (Weapons).

To this day, the importance of Lend-Lease aid to the

Soviet Union during World War II is disputed. The Soviets stopped the German advance and annihilated a German army at Stalingrad when British and American Lend-Lease aid was only a trickle. Some American historians have claimed that the Soviets would have been defeated without the massive aid, and some Soviet historians claim that it was minimal, only equivalent to about 4% of Soviet production. The truth seems to be that Lend-Lease and other aid was indeed important, and the aid probably hastened the German defeat by 12 to 18 months (Weapons).

Soviet and Russian historians have downplayed the significance of Lend-Lease and other support provided by the Allies, but high-ranking officials privately suggested otherwise. In his memoirs, Nikita Khrushchev wrote that without the U.S. aid, the Soviet Union would have lost the war, a belief that he claimed Stalin also shared with him (Coalson). Marshal Georgy Zhukov, the Red Army's foremost leader during the war, was quoted as saying, "Today some say the Allies didn't really help us ... But listen, one cannot deny that the Americans shipped over to us material without which we could not have equipped our armies held in reserve or been able to continue the war."

Lend-Lease was particularly instrumental in terms of communication and transportation. The US and British together sent the Soviets 35,000 radio stations, 380,000 field telephones, and 956,000 miles of telephone cable. The U.S. sent about 1,900 locomotives, far more than the Soviets produced, as well as more than 11,000 boxcars and 56% of the rails used by Soviet railways during the war.

The huge amount and variety of aid sent to the Soviets did not actually win the war, but there can be little doubt that it hastened the Soviet victory. In particular, thanks to hundreds of thousands of American jeeps and trucks, the Red Army in late 1944 and in 1945 was far more mobile and far more capable of a blitzkrieg kind of campaign than the Germans were at the start of the war (Weapons). The Soviet military even marched in American boots, with 15 million pairs of boots sent as part of the aid, and their soldiers were fond of the huge amount of canned meat sent, especially Spam.

Of course, the aid also included sizable quantities of weapon systems. That included providing the Soviets with 13,000 tanks and 14,000 aircraft, as well as 8,000 tractors and other heavy items needed in military construction projects (Coalson). Credible estimates suggest that American supplies routed to the Soviets through the Persian Corridor were sufficient to supply and maintain the equivalent of about 60 American combat divisions (Motter 5). By Soviet standards, American divisions were large and lavishly equipped, so the aid provided was equivalent to well over 60 Red Army divisions. During the war, the Soviet Union fielded something like 500 divisions, which suggests that Lend-Lease was a substantial fraction of the total Soviet war effort.

There was also substantial aid carried to the Persian Gulf ports, but not intended for the Soviets. The British forces in Iran and Iraq had to be supplied, as did the 30,000 American troops, the large number of Polish refugees, and support for the Iranians themselves. The British and Commonwealth troops in Palestine, as well as forces in North Africa, also had to be supplied largely from the Gulf region, until the Mediterranean routes became more secure. The Lend-Lease aid came from the United States, but supplies also came from Australia, New Zealand, South Africa and particularly from India (Motter 5).

All told, an estimated 5,149,376 long tons of aid was shipped through the Persian Corridor, of which some 4,417,243 tons was provided by the Americans. Most of it was shipped to the Soviet Union on U.S. Army-run trucks and trains. The aid was then calculated at a bit over $11 billion, equivalent to several hundred billions in contemporary dollars.

Online Resources

Other World War II titles by Charles River Editors

Further Reading

Army Historical Society. "Railroaders in Olive Drab: The Military Railroad Service in World War II." armyhistory.org/railroaders-in-olive-drab/. Accessed December 8, 2021.

Atabaki, Touraj. "Persia/Iran." International Encyclopedia of the First World War. encyclopedia. 1914-18-online.net/article/persiairan/. Accessed December 10, 2021.

Barni, Robert and John Long. "From Khorramshahr to Kazvin." *Army Transportation Journal* 1 (9), October 1945. 20-22.

Bykofsky, Joseph and Harold Larson. *The Transportation Corps: Operations Overseas. The United States Army in World War II, The Technical Services.* Washington, D.C.: The Center of Military History, 1990.

Coakley, Robert. "The Persian Corridor as a Route for Aid to the U.SS.R." in Kent Greenfield, *Command Decisions*. Washington D.C.: Center of Military History, 2000. 225-254.

Coalson, Robert. "'We Would Have Lost,' Did U.S. Lend-Lease Tip the Balance in Soviet Fight Against Nazi Germany?" Radio Liberty, May 7, 2020. rfel.org/a/did/-lend-lease-aid -tip-the-balance-in-soviet-fight/. Accessed

December 7, 2021.

Encyclopedia Iranica. "Anglo Persian Oil Company." encyclopediairanica.org/articles/ anglo-persian-oil-company/. Accessed December 12, 2021.

Faruqi, Anwar. "Forgotten Polish Exodus to Iran." *Washington Post*, November 23, 2000. washingtonpost.com/archive/2000/11/23/forgotten-polish-exodus/. Accessed December 7, 2021.

Franklin D. Roosevelt Presidential Library. "Lend-Lease." fdrlibrary.org/lend-lease/. Accessed December 7, 2021.

Johnson, Danny. "The Persian Gulf Command and the Lend-Lease Mission to the Soviet Union During World War II." Army History Foundation. Armyhistory.org/the-persian-gulf -command-and-the-lend-lease-mission/. Accessed December 6, 02.

Military History Now. "Gulf War 1941 - The Forgotten Allied Invasion of Iran." November, 2017. militaryhistorynow.com/2017/11/2/iran-vs-the-allies-the-persian-gulf-war-or-1941/. Accessed December 6, 2021.

Motter, T.H. Vail. "The Persian Corridor and Aid to Russia," in *The U.S. Army in World War II, the Middle East Theater.* Washington D.C.: Center of Military History, 1952.

Newel, Clayton. "Railroading in Olive Drab: The Military Railroad Service in World War 2." *On Point*, 19 (2), Fall 2013. 6-13.

O'Sullivan, Adrian. *German Covert Initiatives and British Intelligence in Persia (Iran), 1941-1945*. PhD Dissertation. University of South Africa. researchgate.net/publication/ 320173600/. Accessed December 9, 2021.

Schubert, Frank. "Engineers in the Persian Gulf." The Military Engineer 86 (561), January-February 1994. 252.

Smith, Steven. "Off the Roads: The Forgotten Bastards of Iran." historynet.com/the-battle-before the battle.htm/. Accessed December 6, 2021.

United States Holocaust Museum. "Polish Refugees in Iran During World War II." encyclopedia.ushmm.org/content/en/article/polish-refugees-in-iran/. Accessed December 11, 2021.

Weapons and Warfare. "Lend-Lease to the U.S.S.R." June, 2020. weaponsandwarfare.com/ 2020/06/08/lend-lease-to-U.S.S.R./. Accessed December 8, 2021.

Weital, Mikhail. "Contracting the Persian Corridor." U.S. Army ACC Command. armil/article/ 117265/contracting-in-the-persian-corridor/. Accessed December 9, 2021.

Wynn, Charters. "Lend-Lease." *In Not Even Past*, March, 2020 (online magazine). repositories.lib.utexas.edu/bitstream/handle/2152/8410/lend-lease. Accessed December 9, 2021.

Zimmerman, Dwight. "Lend-Lease to Russia: The Persian Corridor." Defense Media Network, November 8, 2012. defensemedianetwork.com/stories/lend-lwase-to-russia-the-persian-corridor/. Accessed December 6, 2021.

Free Books by Charles River Editors

We have brand new titles available for free most days of the week. To see which of our titles are currently free, click on this link.

Discounted Books by Charles River Editors

We have titles at a discount price of just 99 cents everyday. To see which of our titles are currently 99 cents, click on this link.